Let Us Give

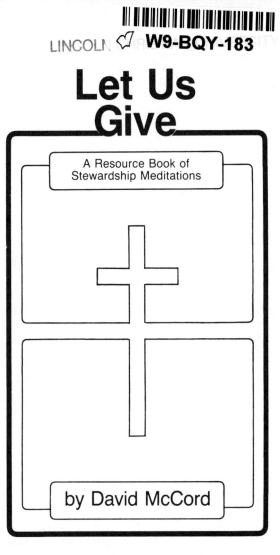

A Resource Book of
Stewardship Meditations

by David McCord

STANDARD PUBLISHING

Cincinnati, Ohio   3024

Scripture quotation are from the *Revised Standard Version* of the Bible.

Library of Congress Cataloging in Publication Data

McCord, David M.
  Let us give.

  1. Stewardship, Christian—Meditations.   I. Title.
BV772.M39   1986   248'.6   86-3723
ISBN 0-87403-098-6

Contents

13001

Preface

Our society tells us that getting is everything. The object of life for many is purely materialistic—accumulate wealth and all that it will buy, and therein you will find happiness.

Our God tells us differently. There is more joy, blessings, and fulfillment in giving than in receiving. This is because wealth and the accumulation of wealth is merely a means to an end—to glorify and serve God and to assist those who are in need.

Money has always been a subject of importance to the Christian faith, and to Judaism before that. Much of our Lord's teachings and parables were on the subject, or related to the subject, of wealth and material possessions. Your religion can either be blocked or facilitated by your wealth and your attitude toward it—that is, whether you love it to have, or have it to use and to give.

Time needs to be taken in our worship services for a stewardship meditation prior to receiving the offering, as more and more churches today are doing. Properly prepared and presented, the stewardship meditation can help the worshiper keep the place of money in worship in its proper perspective; it is a necessary but joyful act of worship.

The ideal stewardship meditation will not only help worshipers to worship, it will also motivate them to give, and provide them with some information or inspiration from God's Word that will help them to be better stewards of God's blessings.

The purpose of this book is to provide stewardship meditations and other helps for those who, from time to time, may be called on to present them in public worship. It is hoped that this material will stimulate your thoughts and help you develop your own meditations. You should feel free to use any of these meditations just as they are written, or adapt them to your personal or group needs.

Stewardship Meditations for Every Lord's Day

Abundance

"If I make a commitment to God to give Him so much each week, how can I be sure that I will have enough to be able to keep that commitment?"

The future is uncertain. I would like to be able to make promises I know I can keep, or else not make any at all. Financially, we just do not know what the future may hold. The economy is fickle and may improve or decline without so much as a moment's notice.

Now, if somehow we could know that we would always have enough of everything, that would be a different matter, wouldn't it? What does God say about this?

"And God is able to provide you with every blessing in abundance, so that you may always have enough of everything and may provide in abundance for every good work" (2 Corinthians 9:8).

God has promised you abundance, not for you to squander, but for you to help meet the needs of the kingdom and of others. Commit your tithes and offerings to God in faith; He will provide for you abundantly.

Date Used: _____

Benevolence

What are you doing to help meet the needs of those who are less fortunate than yourself?

Two young boys were discussing their girl problems. One explained, "I've walked to school with her three times and carried her books. I bought her an ice cream soda twice. Now, do you think I ought to kiss her?"

His friend replied thoughtfully, "Naw, you don't need to. You've done enough for her already."

As long as needs exist, as long as there is human suffering, and as long as there are people in this world who do not know Jesus Christ, we dare not even think that we have done enough.

James writes, "If a brother or sister is ill-clad and in lack of daily food, and one of you says to them, 'Go in peace, be warmed and filled,' without giving them the things needed for the body, what does it profit? So faith by itself, if it has no works, is dead" (James 2:15-17).

In our offerings today we add to our faith our works, the fruits of our labors, that the needs of others may be met.

Date Used: _____

Blessings (1)

Listen to the wisdom of the church through the ages. Perhaps you have heard these statements or some like them many times before.

"It is easier to live on the remaining nine-tenths than it was to live on the ten-tenths before."

"When there was a genuine need, God always provided."

"It is more blessed to give than to receive."

Why do you suppose God has blessed us so abundantly and so consistently? The Psalmist has left us this wise testimony:

"I have been young, and now am old;
    yet I have not seen the righteous forsaken
    or his children begging bread.
He is ever giving liberally and lending,
    and his children become a blessing"
                (Psalms 37:25, 26)

Date Used: _____

Blessings (2)

The Board of Directors of a hospital for the mentally ill were touring the hospital grounds one day, when they came upon a group of patients who were involved in a work project for therapeutic purposes. They were helping to build a brick wall.

One of the directors noticed a patient who was struggling to push a wheelbarrow along upside down. Wanting to be helpful, she suggested, "Wouldn't it be easier if you turned your wheelbarrow over?"

"Not on your life," the patient replied. "I turned it over yesterday and they put bricks in it!"

Some people want their wheelbarrows right side up only to be filled with blessings, but when they see the responsibilities coming, they quickly turn them over.

God wants you to be a part of the work crew in His kingdom, with your wheelbarrow right side up for both reasons. There are responsibilities for you to fulfill and there are blessings for you to receive.

One of your responsibilities is giving to the church. The result will be a wheelbarrow full of blessings.

As the prophet Malachi wrote: "Bring the full tithes into the storehouse, that there may be food in my house; and thereby put me to the test, says the Lord of hosts, if I will not open the windows of heaven for you and pour down for you an overflowing blessing" (Malachi 3:10).

Date Used: _____

Church

The story is told about President Teddy Roosevelt that as a child he was reluctant to go into the church building, especially when it was dimly lit. His parents were understandably concerned about this and eventually got Teddy to explain his reluctance.

He had once heard the preacher quote the Scripture from Psalm 69:9 (KJV), "For the zeal of thine house hath eaten me up . . ." Though he did not know what a "Zeal" was, he knew he did not want to become the meal for a Zeal.

The apostle Paul admonishes those who give aid to do it with zeal (Romans 12:8). Then he adds, "Never flag in zeal, be aglow with the Spirit, serve the Lord" (Romans 12:11).

How zealous are you for the church and for the work of the kingdom?

Date Used: _____

Commitment

An ancient legend tells of a wealthy merchant who was overtaken by a terrible storm while at sea. He vowed fervently to Jupiter that if he were spared he would give him one hundred oxen.

The storm soon subsided and the merchant began to rationalize that surely seven oxen would be sufficient while one hundred was much too extravagant.

Another storm, worse than the first, began to rage. So he promised Jupiter that in exchange for his life he would keep his bargain and the seven oxen would be delivered as promised. As soon as the storm was over and the sea was calm he came down to one ox.

A third, ferocious storm followed, upon which the merchant quickly promised Jupiter that he would not try to deceive him again if he would only deliver him to dry ground. Once ashore he felt safe and secure, and promptly decided that a sheep would be as good an offering as an ox, and much less expensive.

On the way to the temple of Jupiter to offer the sheep he discovered some luscious dates, and decided they should please Jupiter every bit as much as an old sheep would. But he was hungry and ate the dates.

When he finally arrived at the temple, he bowed humbly and placed the pits upon the altar, confident that Jupiter would understand.

When asked what was the first and greatest commandment, Jesus answered: "The first is, 'Hear, O Israel: The Lord our God, the Lord is one; and you shall love the Lord your God with all your heart, and with all your soul, and with all your mind, and with all your strength'" (Mark 12:30).

Commitment to God means honoring Him with all that you have and all that you are, without rationalization and without reduction.

Date Used: _____

Faith

God wants you to walk by faith, to live by faith, and to give by faith.

In the midst of the great roll call of the faithful in the eleventh chapter of Hebrews, this statement is recorded:

"Without faith it is impossible to please him. For whoever would draw near to God must believe that he exists and that he rewards those who seek him" (Hebrews 11:6).

As you present your offering this morning, think on these three truths based on this Scripture:

1. Without faith it is impossible to please God, no matter how much money you may give.

2. Your nearness to God depends on your faith in Him, believing that He exists.

3. And you need to believe and understand that He is a God who rewards those who seek Him.

Date Used: _____

Faithfulness

"Faithful" is one of the names of Jesus (Revelation 19:11). The faithfulness of God is consistently proclaimed and demonstrated throughout Scripture as well as in our daily lives.

I love that beautiful hymn that praises God with the exclamation, "Great is thy faithfulness, O God my Father!" It is based on Lamentations 3:22, 23: "The steadfast love of the Lord never ceases, his mercies never come to an end; they are new every morning; great is thy faithfulness."

You can depend on God! In return, He expects and requires your faithfulness to Him, including your use of riches, as Jesus explained at the conclusion of His parable about the dishonest steward:

"He who is faithful in a very little is faithful also in much; and he who is dishonest in a very little is dishonest also in much. If then you have not been faithful in the unrighteous mammon, who will entrust to you the true riches? And if you have not been faithful in that which is another's, who will give you that which is your own? No servant can serve two masters; for either he will hate the one and love the other, or he will be devoted to the one and despise the other. You cannot serve God and mammon" (Luke 16:10-13).

God is faithful to you. Be faithful to Him.

Date Used: _____

Generosity

God never expects more of you than you are able to do. However rich or impoverished you may be, however great or few your talents, God wants you to do and to give your best.

"The woods would be very silent if only the birds with the sweetest songs were heard."

As we give cheerfully and generously to bless others we find that we are generously blessed.

"One man gives freely, yet grows all the richer; another withholds what he should give, and only suffers want. A liberal man will be enriched, and one who waters will himself be watered" (Proverbs 11:24, 25).

Date Used: _____

Grace

It is by God's grace that we are here today, just as it is by His grace that we are saved.

The grace of God, His unmerited favor and blessings toward us, is both our means and our reason for giving. It is grace that provides for us so that we are able to give, and it is grace that motivates us in our giving.

Paul addresses this fact in 2 Corinthians 9:13-15: "Under the test of this service, you will glorify God by your obedience in acknowledging the gospel of Christ, and by the generosity of your contribution for them and for all others; while they long for you and pray for you, because of the surpassing grace of God in you. Thanks be to God for his inexpressible gift!"

By means of God's grace, and because of God's grace, we offer our gifts to Him today.

Date Used: _____

Investments

Good investments can produce big dividends. God wants us to earn and invest and use what He gives us so that our offerings and sacrifices will be pleasing to Him.

"Not that I seek the gift," writes Paul in Philippians 4, "but I seek the fruit which increases to your credit. I have received full payment, and more; I am filled, having received from Epaphroditus the gifts you sent, a fragrant offering, a sacrifice acceptable and pleasing to God. And my God will supply every need of yours according to his riches in glory in Christ Jesus" (Philippians 4:17-19).

In the parable of the talents, Jesus commended the servants who invested wisely and earned a good return for their master. But for the servant who failed to make any investment, He had these words: "You ought to have invested my money with the bankers, and at my coming I should have received what was my own with interest" (Matthew 25:27).

Hoarding money will worry and condemn you. Investing wisely and using your profits to serve God and help others will bless and reward you.

Date Used: _____

Joy

Is giving a problem for you, or is it a joy? You may have heard the saying, "God loves a cheerful giver even though He also accepts from a church."

Listen to what the Scriptures say about rejoicing and joy.

Deuteronomy 12:6, 7: "And thither you shall bring your burnt offerings and your sacrifices, your tithes and the offering that you present, your votive offerings, your freewill offerings, and the firstlings of your herd and of your flock; and there you shall eat before the Lord your God, *and you shall rejoice*, you and your households, in all that you undertake, in which the Lord your God has blessed you."

Matthew 25:21: "His master said to him, 'Well done, good and faithful servant; you have been faithful over a little, I will set you over much; *enter into the joy of your master.*'"

John 15:8, 11: "By this my Father is glorified, that you bear much fruit, and so prove to be my disciples. . . . These things I have spoken to you, that my joy may be in you, and *that your joy may be full.*"

2 Corinthians 9:7: "Each one must do as he has made up his mind, not reluctantly or under compulsion, *for God loves a cheerful giver.*"

This should be one of the happiest times in our worship service. So put on a big smile, give cheerfully, and experience the joy!

Date Used: _____

Liberality

No matter how poor or how rich you may be, you can give with joy and with liberality, if you will first give yourself. Listen to how Paul commends the churches of Macedonia to the church at Corinth.

"We want you to know, brethren, about the grace of God which has been shown in the churches of Macedonia, for in a severe test of affliction, their abundance of

16

joy and their extreme poverty have overflowed in a wealth of liberality on their part. For they gave according to their means, as I can testify, and beyond their means, of their own free will, begging us earnestly for the favor of taking part in the relief of the saints—and this, not as we expected, but first they gave themselves to the Lord and to us by the will of God" (2 Corinthians 8:1-5).

Date Used: _____

Love

A men well known for his piety died and went to Heaven. As he began to walk through the pearly gates he was abruptly stopped by St. Peter.

"Just a minute," St. Peter said, "you can't just walk in here. You have to have 1,000 points." The man couldn't believe what he was hearing, but St. Peter persisted. "What have you done?"

"Well," the man replied, his mind racing, "I was baptized when I was just a youth and I have faithfully attended church ever since."

"Good!" St. Peter said. "Baptism and church attendance, that's worth one point."

Flabbergasted, and more than a little worried now, the man continued. "I also served the church as a deacon and then later as an elder. And for many years I taught a Sunday School class."

"Wonderful!" exclaimed St. Peter. "Active in church leadership. That now makes a total of two points."

Dismayed, but not ready to give up, the man tried again. "I was faithful in giving my tithes and offerings.

I never missed giving a single Sunday and even made up for the times I was away on vacations."

"Tithes and offerings," St. Peter repeated. "That really is good. You now have a total of three points."

With a sense of utter futility the man cried out, "For the love of God, I don't see how anybody can get in this place!"

"Did I hear you say 'the love of God?' That's an additional nine hundred and ninety seven points!"

Of course, we are not saved by points; we are saved by God's gracious love. "For God so loved the world that he gave his only Son, that whoever believes in him should not perish but have eternal life." (John 3:16)

It is in response to God's love that we offer our gifts of love today.

Date Used: _____

Missions

This congregation is active in missions. A portion of the money you give today will go to help our missionaries in their work. [Here you may wish to name the missionaries you help support.] We are partners with them in the gospel.

Paul recognized this kind of relationship when he wrote to the church at Philippi. "And you Philippians yourselves know that in the beginning of the gospel, when I left Macedonia, no church entered into partnership with me in giving and receiving except you only; for even in Thessalonica you sent me help once and again" (Philippians 4:15, 16).

Why must we give to missions? James S. Stewart in

his book, THINE IS THE KINGDOM, writes: "There is no argument for missions. The total action of God in history, the whole revelation of God in Christ—this is the argument. The one reason for missions is not commission, compassion, community, or continuity. The one reason for missions is Christ. He only is the motive, God's presence in him the one sufficient cause. The church must act because God has acted already."

Let's fulfill our partnership with our missionaries and give generously.

Date Used: _____

Obedience

We talk of "love offerings" and "free will offerings," but do not take this to mean that giving your tithes and offerings to God is somehow optional. It is not. Giving is an act of obedience as well as of love.

"Under the test of this service , you will glorify God by your obedience in acknowledging the gospel of Christ, and by the generosity of your contribution for them and for all others" (2 Corinthians 9:13).

We are too easily distracted by the things of this world and tend to lust after material possessions. But all these things will pass away. It is only through doing God's will, by obedience to Him, that we have eternal life.

Heed John's timely warning: "Do not love the world or the things in the world. If any one loves the world, love for the Father is not in him. For all that is in the world, the lust of the flesh and the lust of the eyes and the pride of life, is not of the Father but is of the world. And the world passes away, and the lust of it; but he who does the will of God abides for ever" (1 John 2:15-17).

Date Used: _____

Planning

Do you find some things to be so confusing you tend to give up on them? Take the game of baseball, for example.

The following explanation appeared in the 1980 Minnesota Twins' program:

You have two sides, one out in the field and one in.

Each man that's on the side that's in goes out and when he's out he comes in and the next man goes in until he's out.

When three men are out the side that's out comes in and the side that's been in goes out and tries to get those coming in out.

Sometimes you get men still in and not out.

When both sides have been in and out nine times including the not outs, that's the end of the game.

Confusing? Sometimes we may feel confused about how to plan our giving. But it really isn't that difficult.

You know how to plan your taxes (and that can really be confusing!), or how to plan to buy a house or a car, or how to plan for a vacation. You can also plan your giving to the church. In fact, God expects you to plan ahead.

That is included in the idea found in 2 Corinthians 9:7: "Each one must do as he has made up his mind, not reluctantly or under compulsion, for God loves a cheerful giver."

Don't wait until Sunday morning, glance in your

wallet or purse, then give God some of the leftovers—if there are any. Instead, plan ahead. Make up your mind what you will give. It is only through planned giving that you can put God first and honor him with your gift.

Date Used: _____

Pledges

Pledging or promising in advance to give an offering to God is a Biblical concept.

For example, the church at Corinth had promised an offering to Paul which they had made a year in advance.

"For I know your readiness, of which I boast about you to the people of Macedonia, saying that Achaia has been ready since last year; and your zeal has stirred up most of them. . . . So I thought it necessary to urge the brethren to go on to you before me, and arrange in advance for this gift you have promised, so that it may be ready not as an exaction but as a willing gift" (2 Corinthians 9:2, 5).

Making a pledge or promise to your church can be helpful to those who, on behalf of the church, must make pledges or promises to others, i.e., to the minister, to missionaries, utility companies, a publishing company, etc.

It also can be a good discipline of faith for you.

Date Used: _____

Possessions

In Luke 12:15 Jesus says: "Take heed, and beware of all covetousness; for a man's life does not consist in the abundance of his possessions."

How timely! It is almost as if Jesus were addressing our American culture. In our super-affluent society the abundance of possessions is the mark of success and happiness. Madison Avenue's philosophy seems to be "If they don't need it, make them think they need it."

The result is that we have become enslaved to buying things that we really don't need but are convinced that we can't live without. We earn to buy to have, and more is better.

Worship helps us to keep things in perspective. We know that what Jesus says is really true, "Life does not consist in the abundance of our possessions." That is slavery.

What life really consists of is loving God and your neighbor as yourself. That is freedom.

Date Used: _____

Priorities

"Honor the Lord with your substance
   and with the first fruits of all your produce;
then your barns will be filled with plenty,
   and your vats will be bursting with wine."

(Proverbs 3:9, 10)

In the business of giving, as well as in the business of living, God has taught us the essential principle of putting Him first: "Thou shalt have no other gods before me."

What takes first place in your life? In the use of your time? In the spending of your money? Is it God? Christ? The church? People in need? Or is it clothes and cars? Food and shelter? Health and pleasure?

It was St. Augustine who said, "Christ is not valued at all unless he is valued above all."

It was Jesus Christ who said, "But seek first his kingdom and his righteousness, and all these things shall be yours as well" (Matthew 6:33).

Date Used: _____

Providence

We worry about having enough food, or clothes, or money. But Jesus says you don't need to worry.

"And why are you anxious about clothing? Consider the lilies of the field, how they grow; they neither toil nor spin; yet I tell you, even Solomon in all his glory was not arrayed like one of these. But if God so clothes the grass of the field, which today is alive and tomorrow is thrown into the oven, will he not much more clothe you, O men of little faith?" (Matthew 6:28-30)

The dictionary gives this definition for the word *providence:* "The foreseeing care and guardianship of God over His creatures." We can't foresee the future, but God can. He will take care of you. You can count on it.

"Every good endowment and every perfect gift is from above, coming down from the Father of lights with whom there is no variation or shadow due to change" (James 1:17).

Date Used: _____

Riches

The Bible never condemns riches, but God does give us some warnings regarding them.

Consider, for example, what Jesus said to the rich young ruler. "How hard it is for those who have riches to enter the kingdom of God! For it is easier for a camel to go through the eye of a needle than for a rich man to enter the kingdom of God" (Luke 18:24, 25).

The problem with riches is that the more you have, the more they tend to interfere with your relationship with God. The more riches you have the more they demand your time and attention. The more possessions you have the more you must maintain them, guard them and tend to them. And if you are busy serving riches, you cannot serve God, for no man can serve two masters.

The problem is eased considerably when we learn to submit our riches to the lordship of Jesus and to the use of the kingdom. When you earn more, give away more. That helps keep riches and religion in perspective.

But can a rich man be saved? The disciples wondered the same thing. "Those who heard it said, 'Then who can be saved?' But he said, 'What is impossible with men is possible with God'" (Luke 18:26, 27).

Date Used: _____

Sacrifice

What would you be willing to give up in order to save your life? Or, more importantly, in order to have eternal life?

Along a rural lane in Korea, American tourists took pictures of a boy who was dragging a plow while an old man guided it along. Later a missionary explained to the group that the family had sold its only ox for money to help build their village church.

We are not good at making sacrifices. For many of us that may mean doing without dessert or missing our favorite television program.

But how many of you are willing to be deprived of comfort or sleep, or to work longer hours or take a second job, or to go hungry and miss a meal or two or three each week, in order to give more money to missions, to the church, and for the needs of others? There is so much we could do to win people to Christ if only we were willing to pay the price of sacrifice.

If you have trouble denying things for yourself, perhaps it is because you have not learned to deny yourself for Him.

Jesus said, "If any man would come after me, let him deny himself and take up his cross and follow me. For whoever would save his life will lose it, and whoever loses his life for my sake will find it" (Matthew 16:24, 25).

Date Used: _____

Security

One of the most famous cliches in the history of man is found on our currency, "In God We Trust."

In fact, we are much more likely to look for security in jobs and businesses, houses and lands, bank accounts and insurance policies, than in God. Yet He is where our true security lies.

It is God who
"prolongs the life of the mighty by his power;
   they rise up when they despair of life.
He gives them security, and they are supported;
   and his eyes are upon their ways"

                              (Job 24:22, 23)

Date Used: _____

Sharing

The rich young ruler was puzzled, just as we often are, by what Jesus told him. "'One thing you still lack. Sell all that you have and distribute to the poor, and you will have treasure in heaven; and come, follow me.' But when he heard this he became sad, for he was very rich" (Luke 18:22, 23).

This was not so much a condemnation or riches as it was of selfishness. However great or small our wealth may be, God wants us to share it to help alleviate the physical and spiritual needs in our world.

James Russell Lowell penned this well-known sentiment:

   "Not what we give, but what we share,

   For the gift without the giver is bare;

   Who gives himself with his alms feeds three,

   Himself, his hungering neighbor, and Me."

In judgment we will be held accountable for how well we released our resources for the needs of others. "And the King will answer them, 'Truly, I say to you, as you did it to one of the least of these my brethren, you did it to me'" (Matthew 25:40).

Date Used: _____

Stewardship

What is a steward? According to the dictionary, a steward is "a person who manages another's property."

According to the Bible, we are to be stewards of God's property, managing it for Him. What does that include?

Psalm 24:1: "The earth is the Lord's and the fulness thereof, the world and those who dwell therein."

Psalms 50:10: "For every beast of the forest is mine, the cattle on a thousand hills."

Haggai 2:8: "The silver is mine, and the gold is mine, says the Lord of hosts."

Romans 14:8: "If we live, we live to the Lord, and if we die, we die to the Lord; so then, whether we live or whether we die, we are the Lord's."

We own nothing. Everything belongs to God. Are you managing your life and your possessions for yourself, or for God?

Romans 14:12: "So each of us shall give account of himself to God."

Date Used: _____

Thanksgiving

Saying "thank you" is a social grace that we teach our children when they are still very young. When others are kind or thoughtful or helpful toward us, we owe them our gratitude and we are motivated to express our thanksgiving to them.

God is so good and has blessed us so bountifully, how can we best express our thanksgiving to Him?

God's Word teaches us that thanksgiving is a product, and that we produce thanksgiving to God through the generosity of our giving.

"You will be enriched in every way for great generosity, which through us will produce thanksgiving to God; for the rendering of this service not only supplies the wants of the saints but also overflows in many thanksgivings to God" (2 Corinthians 9:11, 12).

Date Used: _____

Time

Stewardship involves the management of our time as well as our money.

"Look carefully then how you walk, not as unwise men but as wise, making the most of the time, because the days are evil" (Ephesians 5:15, 16).

How much time should a Christian give to God? As in the case of tithing, the Old Testament law provides us with a minimal example.

"Remember the sabbath day, to keep it holy. Six days you shall labor, and do all your work; but the seventh day is a sabbath to the Lord your God ..." (Exodus 20:8-10).

The Jew committed one day each week wholly to God, one-seventh of his time, fourteen per cent. Can we do any less? "For I tell you, unless your righteousness exceeds that of the scribes and Pharisees, you will never enter the kingdom of heaven" (Matthew 5:20).

We understand that all of life is holy to God, and we are to manage one hundred per cent of our time to His glory. But how much time away from work and your leisure will you commit wholly to God?

Certainly planning one day a week, or its equivalent, for Christian worship and service to the church and to others, is a reasonable place to begin.

Date Used: _____

Tithing

Tithing is giving ten per cent of all that one receives to the Lord.

Someone estimated that in the typical church, if every member was on Social Security and would tithe, the church's income would double or triple. What would we do with all the money if every member gave at least a tithe?

Three youngsters were bragging about their dads' incomes. "My dad is a dentist," said the first. "He drills a little hole, fills it up, and collects fifty dollars."

"My dad is a psychiatrist," said the second. "He talks to a patient for a little while and collects one hundred dollars."

"That's nothing," said the third. "My dad is a minister. He just works one hour on Sunday morning and it takes four men to carry all the money!"

As a matter of fact, our tithes are to be used for the proclamation of the gospel, but not just by the minister. The Old Testament law regarding tithing was for the support of the work of the temple. The tithe has become the minimal example for Christians for the support of the church.

"Do you not know that those who are employed in the temple service get their food from the temple, and those who serve at the altar share in the sacrificial offerings? In the same way, the Lord commanded that

29

those who proclaim the gospel should get their living by the gospel" (1 Corinthians 9:13, 14).

Date Used: _____

Wealth

Friedrich Durrenmatt, in his three-act play, THE VISIT, tells the story of an old woman who was reputedly the wealthiest woman in the world.

She pays a visit to her old hometown, which is now in desperate poverty. She promises the people one million pounds, but on the condition that they murder the man who had been her childhood sweetheart. He had jilted her for another, which she claimed led to her great unhappiness and moral ruin.

In the first act the townspeople abhor the idea. In the second act they begin to buy on credit, liking the idea of having money. And they begin to see how the one-time sweetheart, their fellow townsman, had indeed done the wealthy woman a terrible injustice.

In the third act they actually commit the murder and feel that they are totally justified. Their greed has come to possess them.

This play is meant to be the story of any town, of you and me, and of what can happen when our possessions take charge and we lost control.

Jesus has taught us the true meaning of wealth. "For you know the grace of our Lord Jesus Christ, that though he was rich, yet for your sake he became poor, so that by his poverty you might become rich" (2 Corinthians 8:9).

Date Used: _____

Worship

Giving is an act of worship.

Modern-day man does not understand this. Materialism is his religion and greed is his creed. "It is more blessed to get than to give," he thinks.

Jesus faced this same temptation. "Again, the devil took him to a very high mountain, and showed him all the kingdoms of the world and the glory of them; and he said to him, 'All these I will give you, if you will fall down and worship me.' "Then Jesus said to him, 'Begone, Satan! for it is written,

You shall worship the Lord your God
and him only shall you serve'"
(Matthew 4:8-10).

As we present our tithes and offerings today we are saying "No" to Satan and to his offer to have it all for ourselves. Instead we are worshiping God and reaffirming that He takes first place in our lives and in the stewardship of our money.

Date Used: _____

Stewardship Meditations for Special Days

New Year's Day

We all like new things. But new things become old things so quickly. Christmas toys may be one evidence of that fact.

The idea that each new year we are to begin all over again is a pagan concept. It is like the false doctrine of reincarnation. It says that you did not get it right the first time, you are condemned to try again.

The good news of the gospel of Jesus Christ is that you do not have to keep living your life over until you live it perfectly. Neither do you have to begin again with the coming of each new year.

Instead, God forgives you. When you become a Christian He gives you a clean slate, a new beginning, a new life. Now your relationship with God is eternal, and nothing can separate you from His love.

"I have loved you with an everlasting love," God says. "Therefore I have continued my faithfulness to you" (Jeremiah 31:3b).

In response to God's forgiveness, love and faithfulness, we bring Him our offerings and our lives.

Date Used: _____

Palm Sunday

It was indeed a triumphant entry! Jesus rode like a king on the colt. The people placed their garments in his path, waved the branches of trees and shouted, "Blessed is the King who comes in the name of the Lord! Peace in heaven and glory in the highest!"

"And some of the Pharisees in the multitude said to him, 'Teacher, rebuke your disciples.' He answered, 'I tell you, if these were silent, the very stones would cry out'" (Luke 19:38-40).

Neither can we remain silent. We know that Jesus is indeed the King of kings and the Lord of lords. And as His loyal subjects we pay homage today with songs of praise and with offerings of love, and with the prayer, "Thy kingdom come . . . on earth as it is in heaven."

Date Used: _____

Easter

These are the words of the risen Christ as recorded in Luke 24:46-49.

"Thus it is written, that the Christ should suffer and on the third day rise from the dead, and that repentance and forgiveness of sins should be preached in his name to all nations, beginning from Jerusalem. You are witnesses of these things. And behold, I send the promise of my Father upon you; but stay in the city, until you are clothed with power from on high."

Resurrection! It means that Jesus is indeed the Son of the living God.

Resurrection! It means that Jesus does indeed have the power to forgive sins, and that we are forgiven.

Resurrection! It means that death and sin no more have power over us, and that we shall live forever.

Resurrection! It means that we now have His Spirit living within us, and that we are empowered to be His witnesses.

This offering that we bring this morning is part of our witness: that Jesus is our living Lord, and that we are committed to spreading the good news to all peoples.

Date Used: _____

Mother's Day

Many times has a mother's faith inspired and blessed us.

Once there was a great famine in the land and the people there were on the brink of starvation. A man of God asked a woman, who was a widow as well as a mother, for something to eat. This was her pitiful reply:

"As the Lord your God lives, I have nothing baked, only a handful of meal in a jar, and a little oil in a cruse; and now, I am gathering a couple of sticks, that I may go in and prepare it for myself and my son, that we may eat it, and die" (1 Kings 17:12).

But the prophet Elijah instructed her to feed him first, then herself and her son, assuring her that God would not let her run out of meal or oil until it rained again. She believed Elijah and trusted in God with this result:

"The jar of meal was not spent, neither did the cruse of oil fail, according to the word of the Lord which he spoke by Elijah" (1 Kings 17:16).

What an outstanding example of faith this mother has given us! Put God first. Give Him generously of what you have. And remember that He will never fail you nor forsake you.

Date Used: _____

Memorial Day

Today we remember those who have given their lives that we might be free to live and worship as we choose.

Parents who had lost a son in the war presented a large cash gift to their church in his memory.

Another couple learned of this and the husband suggested they should do the same thing. His wife protested: "But our son came home."

"That is exactly why we should make the gift," he said.

Must we lose much before we give much? Christ has already given His life for us. Let that be our motive for giving today.

"Greater love has no man than this, that a man lay down his life for his friends" (John 15:13).

Date Used: _____

Pentecost

Today is Pentecost, the birthday of the church. Perhaps we should have a party. What would you bring as a gift?

As a matter of fact, the first Christians did respond to the beginning of the church with the bringing of gifts. "And all who believed were together and had all things in common; and they sold their possessions and goods and distributed them to all, as any had need" (Acts 2:44, 45).

The needs of the church today are as great as they ever were. There are people everywhere who are hungry for food and for the word of God.

Let us give generously, and sacrificially, that the world may come to know Christ and become a part of His church.

Date Used: _____

Children's Day/Youth Sunday

Abraham Lincoln said: "Children are the persons who are going to carry on what you have started. They will sit where you are sitting. They will assume control of your cities, states and nations. They will take over your churches, schools, universities and corporations. The fate of humanity is in their hands."

The Bible says: "Train up a child in the way he should go, and when he is old he will not depart from it" (Proverbs 22:6).

The Christian education that you as families, and that we as the church, provide children is essential for the future of their lives and of our world.

36

The offerings you bring today help to provide the care, instruction and inspiration that our children need today, and help to prepare them for tomorrow.

Date Used: _____

Father's Day

Found in a fortune cookie: "You will soon meet a cute brunette. You will give her money. She is our cashier."

That's a pretty safe prediction. Money has a way of getting away from us.

You fathers are constantly concerned about how little money comes in and how much seems to go out. There are so many expenses that soon you begin the old adage "money has wings."

Did you know that is based on a verse in the Bible? Proverbs 23:4, 5 says:
"Do not toil to acquire wealth;
   be wise enough to desist.
When your eyes light upon it, it is gone;
   for suddenly it takes to itself wings,
   flying like an eagle toward heaven."

A wise father will not work for wealth. He will work for his wife and children. He will work for his daily bread. And he will work for the sake of the kingdom.

Date Used: _____

Independence Day

Jack Benny, famous for his frugality, was accosted one day by an armed robber. "Your money or your life," the would-be robber demanded. There was a long silence, but no answer. Impatiently the robber tried again. "I said, your money or your life."

"I'm thinking. I'm thinking," Benny replied.

For most of us that is no decision at all. Life is a precious thing. Our fourth of July holiday may be a time for picnics and parties, but it is also a time to remember our heritage as a nation. We are grateful for those who have given their lives that we might be guaranteed the right to life, liberty, and the pursuit of happiness.

It is in that freedom that we assemble here today to worship our God. But there is a greater freedom still. "For freedom Christ has set us free; stand fast therefore, and do not submit again to a yoke of slavery" (Galatians 5:1). It is in response to that freedom from sin and the law that we bring our gifts today.

Date Used: _____

Labor Day

Work is sacred. It is also essential.

Paul wrote to the Thessalonians: "If any one will not work, let him not eat. . . . Now such persons we command and exhort in the Lord Jesus Christ to do their work in quietness and to earn their own living" (2 Thessalonians 3:10, 12).

The purpose of work, however, is not a selfish one. We work to serve others, to serve God, and to provide not only for our families but for others as well. God has also taught us compassion for those who cannot work and are genuinely in need.

A plaque carries this inscription: "No one is useless

who lightens the burdens of others." If you use your blessings, whether your work or your money, for the sake of others, you can be sure that God will bless you in return.

As Paul explained to the church at Corinth: "I do not mean that others should be eased and you burdened, but that as a matter of equality your abundance at the present time should supply their want, so that their abundance may supply your want, that there may be equality. As it is written, 'He who gathered much had nothing over, and he who gathered little had no lack'" (2 Corinthians 8:13-15).

Date Used: _____

Thanksgiving

Giving is one of the purest forms of thanksgiving.

It is a natural response to give gifts to those who have given gifts to us, who love and care for us, who help and support us. It is our way of giving substance and meaning to the words "thank you."

We respond to God with our love because He first loved us. We respond to Him with our giving and our thanksgiving because He first gave to us: the gift of His only begotten Son. "Thanks be to God for his inexpressible gift!" (2 Corinthians 9:15).

"Offer to God a sacrifice of thanksgiving,
    and pay your vows to the Most High;
and call upon me in the day of trouble;
    I will deliver you, and you shall glorify me"
                                    (Psalms 50:14, 15)

Date Used: _____

Christmas

Christmas is a time for giving!

It was initiated by God who gave us the precious gift of His own sweet Son, our Savior, on Christmas Day.

It was perpetuated by the Wise-men from the east who brought their treasures of gold and frankincense and myrrh, offering them as gifts of worship to the Christ child.

It has been traditionalized by the story of St. Nicholas, a bishop of Myra in Asia Minor during the fourth century, whose reputation for generous giving lives on today.

It continues to be memorialized today whenever families gather around Christmas trees and share their gifts of love with one another.

The best Christmas verse of all is not even a part of the Christmas story. It is this: "For God so loved the world that he gave his only Son, what whoever believes in him should not perish but have eternal life" (John 3:16).

The third verse of the Christian hymn, "As With Gladness Men of Old," says it very well:

> "As they offered gifts most rare
> At that manger rude and bare,
> So may we with holy joy,
> Pure and free from sin's alloy,
> All our costliest treasures bring,
> Christ, to Thee, our heavenly King."

Date Used: _____

Stewardship Meditations for Special Occasions

Commitment/Pledge Sunday

Proverbs 11:28 says,
"He who trusts in his riches will wither,
but the righteous will flourish like a green leaf."

We trust money too much. We seem to be under the illusion that it will give us security. Actually God is our security, and He is the one in whom we need to put our trust and our faith.

"Each one must do as he has made up his mind, not reluctantly or under compulsion, for God loves a cheerful giver. And God is able to provide you with every blessing in abundance, so that you may always have enough of everything and may provide in abundance for every good work" (2 Corinthians 9:7, 8).

Now is the time to make up your mind to trust God and to put Him first.

How many times have you said, "I will begin putting God first, or living for Him, or giving a tithe, just as soon as I . . ." and then you begin making excuses.

Faith means trusting God to make possible what for you is impossible, and to provide for you what you cannot do for yourself. God understands perfectly your limitations as well as your capabilities, and He is willing to take you just as you are.

Moses gave to God his faltering tongue, David his unclean hands, and Amos his untrained mind. The widow at the temple gave her mite, Paul his imperfect health, and Peter his simple fisherman's strength and faith.

What do you have to give? Whatever it may be, commit it to God in faith.

Date Used: _____

Dedication of a New Building

God commanded King David to build an altar for Him on the threshing floor of Araunah the Jebusite. When Araunah found out David wanted to buy his threshing floor and why he wanted it, he said to David, "Let my lord the king take and offer up what seems good to him; here are the oxen for the burnt offering, and the threshing sledges and the yokes of the oxen for the wood. All this, O king, Araunah gives to the king" (2 Samuel 24:22, 23).

What a bargain! Everything David needed—the threshing floor, the oxen and even the wood—could all be his without cost.

David's reply to Araunah is remarkable if not surprising: "No, but I will buy it of you for a price; I will not offer burnt offerings to the Lord my God which cost me nothing" (2 Samuel 24:24).

This beautiful building is a place where we can learn

and worship and make our offerings to God. It has been made possible at great cost and considerable sacrifice. But we would not have it any other way.

The One who paid the supreme sacrifice on the cross for our sins is worthy of our very best. Let us give our offerings of love and sacrifice today as we help provide this place of worship to His glory.

Date Used: _____

Men's Fellowship

A man was working in the yard of his attractive, ranch-style home located in an affluent new suburb, when a stranger drove up. He parked his car and got out, looked the house over carefully, then walked up to the owner.

"Nice looking house," the stranger said. "Must be worth at least $95,000."

The owner straightened up and retorted, "It's worth $125,000 if it's worth a penny! Why? Are you looking for a house to buy?"

"No," the stranger replied, "I'm the new tax assessor."

We tend to overvalue materials possessions and to treasure things. Jesus promised to give us an entire kingdom if we will just learn to put things aside and put Him first.

Jesus said, "Fear not, little flock, for it is your Father's good pleasure to give you the kingdom. Sell your possessions, and give alms; provide yourselves with purses that do not grow old, with a treasure in the heavens that does not fail, where no thief [or tax assessor!] approaches and no moth destroys. For where your treasure is, there will your heart be also" (Luke 12:32-34).

This men's organization is an important arm of God's kingdom. Let's show that our heart is in the right place by the offering we now give.

Date Used: _____

Musical Concert

"Through him [Jesus] then let us continually offer up a sacrifice of praise to God, that is, the fruit of lips that acknowledge His name. Do not neglect to do good and to share what you have, for such sacrifices are pleasing to God" (Hebrews 13:15, 16).

This beautiful musical presentation has truly been a sacrifice of praise to God, pleasing to Him and to all of us. As you have shared your gifts with us, we now present our offerings to share with you, for the support and continuance of this important ministry.

Date Used: _____

Ordination Service

An admirer of a reknowned concert violinist, wanting to compliment him, said, "I would give my life to be able to play like that."

The violinist replied, "I did."

The one who is ordained here today has made a total commitment of his/her life to Jesus Christ. Yet that is exactly what God expects of each of us. It is just that we have different gifts and are called upon to minister in different ways.

Peter writes: "As each has received a gift, employ it for one another, as good stewards of God's varied grace ..." (1 Peter 4:10).

As part of our stewardship we now bring our tithes and offerings, committed with our lives unto God, for the preaching of the gospel and for winning the world to Christ.

Date Used: _____

Revival Services

Galatians 6:6 says: "Let him who is taught the word share all good things with him who teaches."

We come now to this offering time to share our gifts with the one who has shared with us.

There is a little parable about two water buckets. They were being carried to the well to be filled again.

The first complained, "I don't get it. No matter how many times I am filled at the well I am soon empty again."

The second said, "I think it's just wonderful. No matter how many times I go empty to the well I am always refilled."

Again we have been filled. And soon we will go to our homes and jobs and schools and neighborhoods so that we can share with others the blessings we have received.

Galatians 6 continues: "Do not be deceived; God is not mocked, for whatever a man sows, that he will also reap. For he who sows to his own flesh will from the flesh reap corruption; but he who sows to the Spirit will from the Spirit reap eternal life. And let us not grow weary in well-doing, for in due season we shall reap, if we do not lose heart. So then, as we have opportunity, let us do good to all men, and especially to those who are of the household of faith" (Galatians 6:7-10).

Date Used: _____

Special Offering Project

There are so many demands today on our finances that it is hard to keep up with them all.

A clever statement appeared in the *Changing Times* magazine. It said, "Separation of church and state could hardly be more complete. The church teaches us that money isn't everything and the government keeps telling us it is."

And it looks like the government is winning the argument. The dollar continues shrinking due to taxes, government spending and inflation. Coupled with the commercial pressures to buy more things, very little is left. And God gets the leftovers!

It used to be the problem of keeping up with the Joneses. Now, according to Marshall McLuhan in his book, UNDERSTANDING MEDIA, it is a matter of "keeping *upset* with the Joneses."

Money pressures result when we focus upon the world and the things of the world instead of upon Christ. We need to get our priorities straight.

Paul writes, "Therefore be imitators of God, as beloved children. And walk in love, as Christ loved us and gave himself up for us, a fragrant offering and sacrifice to God" (Ephesians 5:1, 2).

This special offering represents the work of the kingdom, so we can give to it generously and cheerfully.

And we do it in the faith and confidence that He who gave himself for us will also meet our every need.

Date Used: _____

Women's Fellowship

The roll call of women faithful in the work of the Lord is both long and impressive. Just to name a few— Miriam, Esther, Ruth, Deborah, Mary, Elizabeth, Lydia, and Phoebe.

The quiet, simple, hard-working faith of women has often gone unheralded. Sir James M. Barrie said it well: "Every man who is high up likes to think that he has done it all himself, and the wife smiles and lets it go at that."

Women get things done. A rural church in North Carolina was badly in need of a new building. The men argued and debated about the need and the cost and the work was delayed. One day the women of the church met at the building site with their wheelbarrows and shovels and began digging a foundation. The building was soon under construction!

God takes notice. "And he [Jesus] sat down opposite the treasury, and watched the multitude putting money into the treasury. Many rich people put in large sums. And a poor widow came, and put in two copper coins, which made a penny. And he called his disciples to him, and said to them, "Truly, I say to you, this poor widow has put in more than all those who are contributing to the treasury. For they all contributed out of their abundance; but she out of her poverty has put in everything she had, her whole living" (Mark 12:41-44).

What we do as women through this organization

may seem insignificant to some, but God takes notice. That is why in this offering, as in everything that we do, we must give Him our very best.

Date Used: _____

Preparing to Present
a Stewardship Meditation

The person who has been chosen to present a stewardship meditation has also been chosen to be a worship leader. This is certainly an honor and a privilege, but it is also an awesome responsibility.

During these few moments in the worship service all eyes are upon the one presenting the meditation, all ears eagerly await what is to be said. For the most part these worshipers have come to hear God's Word, not merely to be entertained or to pass the time.

What you say and how you say it are important. Careful planning and prayerful preparation need to precede this time. What is the purpose and place of the stewardship meditation in the worship service? How long should it be? How can one best develop his own meditation or personalize a printed meditation he plans to use? What personal preparations are appropriate? Here are some ideas you will find helpful.

The Purpose and Place of
the Stewardship Meditation

Attending some worship services you might get the impression that the offering time was either an afterthought or a necessary evil. As a matter of fact, it is an integral part of one's worship experience and responsibility. Giving, thanksgiving, worship and praise all go together.

The offering time should be a meaningful and joyous part of our worship services. A well thought out and carefully prepared stewardship meditation can help it to be just that. The person who presents the meditation is the key to accomplishing this.

The purpose of the stewardship meditation is to help prepare the worshiper for presenting his tithes and offerings to the Lord. It should help him to perceive his giving in the context of worship, rather than as an interruption to it.

It should help direct his thinking toward God and toward his own responsibility of building up the church, caring for the needy, and evangelizing the world. It should inspire him to think big and to give generously. It should help put a smile on his face and joy in his heart.

The place of the stewardship meditation and offering in the worship service may vary considerably. A suggested order of service would include preceding it with a hymn, preferably on the same theme as the meditation (love, joy, sacrifice, etc.), followed by the meditation, a prayer of praise and thanksgiving, and the receiving of the offering accompanied by instrumental or vocal music.

The Length of the
Stewardship Meditation

The timing of the various parts of a worship service are important. That is becoming more and more true in our time-conscious, impatient society. There is a direct relationship between attention span and effective communication.

How long should a stewardship meditation be? Usually one to three minutes is sufficient to accomplish your purpose and address your topic. This may vary from congregation to congregation, and even from Sunday to Sunday, depending on several factors.

1. *Time allotment.* A specific amount of time may be assigned for this part of the worship service. If this is true, be sure to honor it.

2. *Expectancy of the congregation.* If there is a traditional expectation among the people, it must be considered. If they are expecting a one-minute meditation and it lasts for five minutes, you will surely lose their attention. The opposite may also be true: too short may be as critical an error as too long.

3. *Direction of the minister.* The minister, or whoever presides over the worship service, may have a preferred amount of time in mind for each part of the service. If you are at all uncertain about this it would be good to check with him before your preparations have gone too far.

4. *Special days/offerings.* In the case of a special offering or a special stewardship emphasis, using more time than usual may be warranted. However, this should be coordinated with the other worship leaders involved so there are no surprises.

Personalizing a Stewardship Meditation

With a minimal amount of effort you can greatly improve on the written meditations found in this book or any other. It is seldom satisfactory just to read from a book to an audience, unless you are an exceptionally good reader.

If you do prefer to read the meditation, or perhaps find it necessary to do so, then prepare by reading it several times in advance so that you are thoroughly familiar with it. Make sure that you can pronounce all the words and that the flow of the sentences and thoughts make sense to you. It is even a good idea to read the material aloud so you really get the feel of it.

Adapting or rewriting the meditation is an excellent way of personalizing it or making it your own. A meditation that you have put into your own words will be easier to present and better received and understood by your audience.

Changing words or whole sentences is perfectly acceptable. So is combining sentences or ideas from different meditations. You may want to use different Scriptures or cut down on the amount of Scripture used. You might even want to add an illustration of your own. Just be careful of your time if you are adding material.

Developing Your Own Stewardship Meditation

The best and most interesting stewardship meditations that I have heard are those that were original with the presenter. Developing your own stewardship meditation is not difficult and the results can be most rewarding, for you and for your audience.

Here are some simple steps to follow:

1. *Choose your topic or theme.* What will you talk about? You may discover a stewardship theme you wish to address from your own personal Bible reading or other reading, from this book or others like it, or from special needs that you perceive exist in your congregation.

2. *Decide on your Scripture.* Scripture does not always need to be included, but it does assure you and your audience that what is being said is a word from God and not just your own opinion. Select Scriptures that correspond with your topic or theme by using a topical Bible concordance or those suggested by this book.

Of course, you may select your Scripture first and let that determine what your topic or theme will be.

3. *Incorporate other material you want to use.* You may include a quotation from a book you have read, or from a magazine article, that you would like to use. Or you may include a story you have heard, an incident from Scripture you might want to retell, or an experience from your own life. Do a little creative thinking.

4. *Make your point.* What is it that you really want to say about your topic or theme? What is the point of your Scripture or the story you will tell? You may want your hearers to give more generously, learn sacrifice, repent of selfishness, find joy in obedience, or meet a goal. Be specific and clear regarding the point of your meditation.

5. *Outline what you plan to say.* In other words, organize your notes and your ideas. What will you say first, second, and so on? You might want to try the

following format for your outline or develop your own.

THEME: Priorities. What is most important in your life? You can tell by how you spend your money.

ILLUSTRATION: My son saved money and bought a car. Many hours of work. Very important part of his life. Joy and pride of ownership. His heart was really in it.

SCRIPTURE: "For where your treasure is, there will your heart be also" (See Matthew 6:19-21).

POINT: Put God first in the giving of your time and treasure. This helps make Him first and most important in all things in your life.

6. *Write out your meditation.* This is not absolutely necessary but can give you added security in knowing exactly what you will say and how long it will take you to say it. Writing out your meditation is a good discipline that you may wish to use at first, although later you may wish to use only your outline to speak from.

Personal Preparation

As a worship leader you will communicate not only with your words but also by your attitude and through your appearance. Consider these timely tips on personal preparation that will help you do a better job presenting your stewardship meditation.

1. *Plan what you will say.* Have it written out, outlined, or at least well thought out in advance.

2. *Practice giving your meditation.* Read it or give it one or more times out loud so that you feel ready and confident.

3. *Time your meditation.* This is one of the advantages of giving it aloud in advance. See how long it takes; you may need to do some cutting.

4. *Meditate on God's Word.* Let God speak to you before you attempt to speak on His behalf to others.

5. *Pray about your meditation.* Before you begin, while you are preparing, when you get up to speak, pray. Stay close to Him in prayer throughout the week and you will be much better prepared to present your meditation on Sunday.

6. *Get plenty of rest.* Don't exhaust yourself if you can help it, or stay up too late Saturday night. Go to your task physically refreshed.

7. *Check your appearance.* Neatness enables you to be less conspicuous and to draw people's attention to God rather than to yourself.

8. *Check your attitude.* You don't need to try to be something or someone your are not. Be yourself, but be your best self. Make sure what you say is what you personally believe and practice. Pray for a spirit of integrity and humility.

Scripture Resources for Stewardship Meditations

These Scriptures are included here for you to read and use in developing your own stewardship meditations. They are categorized according to the themes used in the section titled "Stewardship Meditations for Every Lord's Day."

You may also use these Scriptures for your personal reading and devotions. The more you meditate on what God has to say about the stewardship of giving, the more prepared you should be to develop and present your meditation.

Some of these Scriptures have already been used in the meditations that appear in this book. Others have not. This list is not intended to be exhaustive in the use of the themes nor in the Scriptures cited. You will discover others in your studies that will be just as useful or poignant.

Abundance: Luke 12:15; John 10:10; 2 Corinthians 9:8-10; Philippians 4:11-13

Benevolence: Matthew 25:40; Luke 18:22, 23; Acts 4:32-35; 2 Corinthians 9:11, 12; Galatians 6:7-10; James 2:15-17; 1 John 3:16-18; (see also "Sharing")

Blessings: Psalms 37:25, 26: Malachi 3:8-10; 2 Corinthians 9:8

Church: Acts 2:43-45; 3:1-10; 5:1-11; Romans 12:4-8; 1 Corinthians 14:12

Commitment: Psalms 37:3-5; Luke 10:25-28; Romans 12:1, 2

Faith: Matthew 6:33; Mark 6:7-13; 9:23; Luke 12:22-31; 18:24-27; Hebrews 11:6; James 4:13-15

Faithfulness: Psalm 117; Lamentations 3:22, 23; Luke 16:10-13

Generosity: Proverbs 11:24, 25; 2 Corinthians 9:13 (see also "Liberality")

Grace: Proverbs 12:1, 2; John 1:16; Romans 12:6-8; 2 Corinthians 9:13-15; 12:8-10; Ephesians 1:7, 8

Investment: Psalms 62:10; Matthew 25:14-30; Luke 6:37, 38; Galatians 6:7

Joy: Deuteronomy 12:6, 7; Matthew 25:21; Luke 18:18-23; John 15:8-11; 2 Corinthians 9:7

Liberality: Proverbs 11:24, 25; John 12:3-8; Romans 12:6-8; 2 Corinthians 8:1-5 (see also "Generosity")

Love: Jeremiah 31:3b; Luke 10:27; John 3:16; Romans 13:8-10; 2 Corinthians 8:24; Ephesians 5:1, 2; 2 Timothy 1:7; 1 John 2:15-17; 4:19-21

Missions: Acts 16:9, 10; Romans 10:14-17; Philippians 4:14-19

Obedience: Matthew 5:20; 22:15-22; Luke 12:41-48; 16:10-13; John 15:8-11; 2 Corinthians 9:13; 1 John 2:15-17

Planning: 1 Corinthians 16:2; 2 Corinthians 9:6, 7

Pledge: 2 Corinthians 8:10-12; 9:2, 5

Possessions: Isaiah 55:1-3; Matthew 19:21, 22; Luke 12:15; Acts 2:44, 45

Priorities: Exodus 23:19a; Proverbs 3:9, 10; Matthew 6:33; John 2:13-16; 2 Corinthians 8:1-5

Providence: Matthew 6:25-33; Luke 18:28-30; 2 Corinthians 9:8; Philippians 4:19; James 1:17

Riches: Proverbs 11:28; 22:7; Jeremiah 17:11; Matthew 13:22; Luke 12:16-21; 18:24-27; 2 Corinthians 8:9; 1 Timothy 6:17-19; James 2:1-5; Revelation 2:8, 9 (see also "Wealth")

Sacrifice: 2 Samuel 24:21-24; 1 Kings 17:8-16; Matthew 16:24-26; Mark 12:41-44; John 15:12, 13; 2 Corinthians 8:3-5; 8:9; Hebrews 13:16

Security: Job 24:22, 23; Psalms 4:5-8; 1 Thessalonians 5:3

Sharing: Proverbs 22:9; Ecclesiastes 5:13; Luke 12:32-34; 2 Corinthians 8:13-15; Galatians 6:2 (see also "Benevolence")

Stewardship: Psalms 24:1; 50:10, 11; Haggai 2:8; Matthew 6:19-21; Luke 6:37, 38; 12:41-48; 16:1-9; 16:10-13; Romans 14:8, 12; 1 Corinthians 4:1, 2

Thanksgiving: Psalms 50:14, 15; 95:1-7; 105:1-5; 106:1; 2 Corinthians 9:11, 12; 1 Thessalonians 5:18

Time: Exodus 20:8; Ephesians 5:15, 16; Colossians 4:5

Tithe: Genesis 14:18-20; 28:18-22; Leviticus 27:30-34; Malachi 3:10; Matthew 6:20; 23:23; Luke 18:9-14; 1 Corinthians 9:13, 14

Wealth: Proverbs 23:4, 5; Luke 16: 14, 15; 22:3-6; 1 Timothy 6:6-10; Hebrews 11:26; 13:5 (see also "Riches")

Worship: Exodus 20:1-3; Matthew 2:10, 11; 4:8-10; 6:19-21; Romans 12:1; 1 Corinthians 6:19, 20; Ephesians 5:1, 2